Kids' Party
PLANNER
great ideas for fun party themes

FOLD

Kids' Party

PLANNER

great ideas for fun party themes

by Marion Haslam

Easter Bonnet template

See page 49

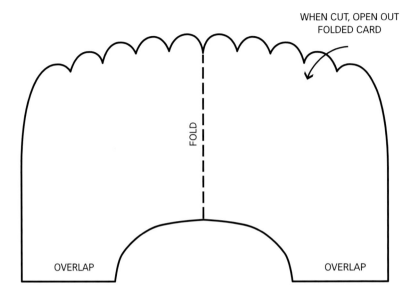

WHEN CUT, OPEN OUT
FOLDED CARD

FOLD

OVERLAP   OVERLAP

Instructions:

1. Re-draw or photocopy the large template on the next page to 200% size.

2. Fold a piece of card and place the edge marked 'fold' along the folded edge.

3. Cut out the shape.

4. Bring the two edges marked 'overlap' together and staple to form the bonnet shape.

5. Decorate as desired!

STAPLE

contents

Totem templates

See page 35

Bear totem template
Scale up as required

Eagle totem template
Scale up as required

Slotted back attachment
Scale up as required
Attach to Eagle and Bear templates

Big Chief totem template
Scale up as required

Children's Parties

Inspirational ideas for planning a fabulous party

Paper Pirate Hat

See page 18

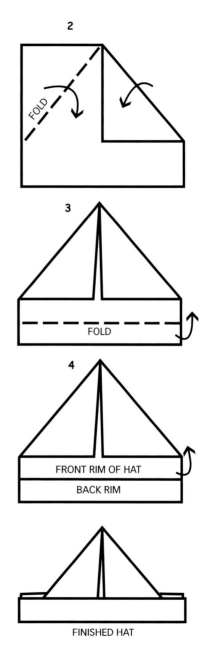

Folding instructions:

Use a sheet of newspaper (tabloid size) or black art paper 37 x 58cm (15in x 23in).

1. Fold the paper in half vertically, turn and then fold again.

2. On the folded edge, fold in a triangle of paper to the centre.

3. Fold up the top layer of paper only, at the base of the hat to meet the folded triangles.

4. Fold up again. Repeat with the other side.

Party inspiration

Whether you view birthday parties as the social event of your year or an occasion to be survived probably depends on whether you are the child involved or the obliging parent organizing the whole event! However, with some inspiration and a little lateral thinking, some help from the intended party person and a high degree of forward planning, parties can be enjoyed by all involved.

Pirate party

This book should be regarded as your saviour and stress-remover! The following pages give some useful hints and tips on forward planning. With ideas galore for themed parties, each theme has suggestions for fantastic party food, easy-to-make (or adapt) costumes, invitations, games and ideas for setting the scene. You can follow this basic 'recipe' for any theme you think up. Help and ideas from your child should be welcomed at this stage with open arms. Children love to feel involved and are sure to have bright ideas of their own. After all, they are princesses and pirates on a daily basis! Plus, from a practical point of view, they can help with the preparation of invitations or table settings well in advance of the actual day.

As you know, for children the countdown to a birthday starts about three months in advance of the actual date, as soon as they pass the magical $3/4$ mark each year. So why not harness some of their boundless energy when it gets to about birthday minus 6 weeks? After all, you are going to hear about it non-stop anyway?

Princess parties and super sleepovers

Cross bones

See page 19

Scale up as required

Cut bones at an angle and slip behind skull (longer bones at the base of the skull)

Party planning hints will help you to create a birthday battle plan and it can be helpful to record ideas for future years. In my family, the exercise book containing details of my parties as a small child is much treasured (and slightly battered), as it records the important events in my own family's history. So, parents, pour yourself a glass of wine as you sit back and read through. On the great day you will be prepared for anything and can relax and enjoy the experience.

Wild west party

Arty party

Sensational summer parties

Templates

Jolly Roger skull
See page 19

Scale up as required

Planning the Perfect Party

OK, let's get one thing straight — parties don't have to be perfect in order to be fabulous, memorable and a great deal of fun.

The main thing to remember is that everyone is there to have a good time, maybe dress up, play some games, get over-excited, eat some food and if you are lucky, calm down a little before they disappear off home again.

Of course, events and activities cannot (and should not) be planned with the precision of a business conference, but a little forethought saves stress (yours) and tears (theirs) on the big day. Thinking ahead also means children's parties need not be expensive, as creative home-based and home-made parties will often contain the most original and memorable ideas. After all, anyone can go to a burger restaurant on their special day, but how many children can celebrate on the Jolly Roger and walk the plank?

Location, location, location

Countdown Planning

With a little forward planning, on the big day you can concentrate on fun rather than organization.

Throughout the year

• Buy seasonal partyware in the sales to save money. Start up a party box and stockpile small gifts or give-aways for goody bags. Remnants of exotic fabrics, nets and trimmings can also be stored for fancy dresses. A materials box with crêpe paper, sticky tape, string, balloons and a pump is also useful as a standby.
• Note down ideas for themes – get inspiration from children's books, films and magazines.

Six weeks before

• Decide on the date and time for the party and theme if applicable. Remember the party doesn't have to be on the actual birthday.
• Book outside venues/entertainers if necessary (you may need longer for popular choices).

Four weeks before

• Decide on the party guests.
• Make and write the invitations. For younger children, print the party details and let them write in the guest's name and sign it. Include your telephone number for RSVPs and a deadline for replying.

PARTY RECORD

Keep a party record in a notebook for useful reference. Include details of themes, games, numbers of guests, party food and other bright ideas that you can use again in future years.

Two – Three weeks before

• Hand out or post the invitations.
• Start making any props or costumes.
• Rope in the help of grandparents or creative friends. Children love playing make believe with extra stand-ins, especially when they are in character (Sheriff and Big Chief Bread-and-Butter for example).
• Buy small prizes or raid your party box.
• Decide on the birthday cake.
• Decide what type of food you will have. Remember to keep it simple, have small portions and consider any allergies (nuts etc).

One week before

• Phone any guests who haven't replied (children do tend to put invitations into their school backpacks and not tell anyone until the day before the party!).
• Buy all non-perishable party food, drink and candles.
• Buy or record any special music you need. With any musical games, have a pre-recorded tape prepared, so there are no gaps as the tracks change.
• Assemble goody bags.

On the morning
(or day before if possible)
• Try to get the birthday child out of the way for a few hours as you'll work a lot faster!
• Decorate your home, garden and tea table.
• Gather together any props you need for the games.
• Prepare food.

THINGS TO THINK ABOUT

How old is the birthday girl or boy? This may seem obvious to you the parent, but what you plan for a five year old can be seen as deeply un-cool for their eight-year-old sibling.

Numbers

Much as little Molly would like to invite her entire class of thirty 'close' friends, think of your sanity and ability to act as a sheep dog. Manageable numbers are generally calculated as the age of the child plus one or two extras. When having a party for the under-threes, this rule can be disregarded as long as each toddler is accompanied by a parent. Bear in mind that if your themed party involves team games or make believe, you may need to increase the guest numbers accordingly to an easily divisible number, such as eight.

Toddlers

For toddlers, of two or three, a party is more for your benefit as a get together with other parents or your immediate family or godparents. Activities are no more high brow than playing with balloons (not letting them touch the ground), bouncing balls, dancing to Ring o' Roses or playing with their favourite toys.

Pre-School age

At four or five, most children will have a wider circle of friends as they start play school or proper school. Parties start to assume great importance in their hectic social whirl. Such parties are probably best at home where there will be plenty of distractions.

Age six to eight

From about the age of six or seven, expect and encourage greater involvement from your child. These can be really fun years as children's imaginations go into overdrive. Their social skills also improve, so you can guarantee a couple of hours of high spirits and frenzied activity. Your home, garden or the local church/village hall are all ideal – having plenty of space at this age to burn off some energy (theirs, not yours) is vital.

Older children

From the age of nine or ten, it is really important to consider the child's likes and dislikes. At this age, activity-type parties out of doors or in another location (swimming pools or sports centres) can be a good option. Another alternative is to invite a small group of friends over for a 'girls-night-in' and a sleepover.

Newton's law

Hang some apples (use windfalls) on strings from the ceiling. Divide the players into pairs and give one player in each team some scissors and the other player a hat. The first player in each pair cuts the apple string and the second player tries to catch it in the hat. The difficulty is that players cannot lift the hat off the floor! The pair which manages to gather the greatest number of apples wins the game. If played outside, tie the strings to trees or the washing line.

Spooky shadows

This is a good game for quietening everyone down before eating or leaving. Attach a white sheet on one wall. One of the children sits down on a chair facing the sheet. At the opposite wall of the room is a lamp on the table. All the players walk between the lamp and the guesser in turn. The guesser must recognize the players by their shadows (he/she must not turn around). The players try to change their shadows by hunching their shoulders, stooping or changing their appearance with a hat or false beard. The player who is recognized becomes the guesser in the following round. You can also play traditional shadow miming games.

The witch's relay

Divide the guests into two teams and have half of each team at either end of the room. The first player puts one of his/her feet into an empty bucket. Holding the bucket handle in one hand and a broom or besom in the other, the player must run to the other side of the room – it's harder than it looks! – and then pass the bucket and broom onto the next player. The first team to finish is the winner.

Carving pumpkins

These giant fruit are a traditional part of the Halloween fun (and food). Available in all shapes and sizes, they can be hollowed out and lit from the inside with a tea light. You must ask an adult to help you.

• First draw a simple design of eyes, nose and mouth on one side with a felt tip pen and a circle at the top.

• Ask an adult to cut out the top of the pumpkin and the outlines of the shapes using a small, sharp vegetable knife or craft knife.

• Circles can be easily created with an apple corer.

• Scoop out the flesh with an ice-cream scoop or melon baller.

• The flesh can be used for pumpkin soup or pies and the seeds toasted.

• Line up pumpkins in the window or on the garden path for a welcoming glow.

Goody bags

Use squares of black felt or crêpe paper, quickly sewn or glued into sacks. Fill with any small gifts in suitable colours, plus an apple and orange. Other treats could include jellied monsters and lips, DIY wands, some awful jokes, plus craft materials for making pom pom spiders and pipe cleaner specs.

Timing

Two to two-and-a-half hours is plenty for older children. Believe me! It is amazing what you can fit in to this length of time. Unlike adults, children don't need to 'warm up'. They are raring to go the moment they arrive. Any longer and the birthday boy or girl will be running on empty and tempers are likely to get frayed. Far better to go out on a high and leave the guests wanting more.

Good ice breaker

SNAP! Using a packet of Snap playing cards, which are extremely cheap, hide half around the house and garden (some obvious, others more hidden) with a small wrapped sweet or chocolate coin attached to the back. Divide the other half amongst the guests as they arrive. Set them off looking for their matching pair.

Suggested party breakdown

It's useful to have a running order to ensure the party progresses smoothly and to avoid those 'what shall we do next' moments.

First 30 minutes

Guests arrive – have an immediate activity that they can all join in, such as decorating a plate or place card holder. If it's a costume party, have a dressing-up station and another adult on hand to act as wardrobe mistress.

Next 60 minutes

Structured games and play

Next 30 minutes

Birthday tea

Next 30 minutes

Quiet games, present opening and giving out of party bags

The other essential part of timing is to put a time limit on some activities and to alternate competitive and non-competitive games. Pass the Parcel for five to ten minutes is fun; stretch it to twenty and everyone will be getting fidgety. It is a far better idea to repeat an activity in another guise later. Try to arrange it so that everyone wins a small prize.

Setting the scene

• Use coloured card from art shops or crêpe paper, folded into zigzags and make garlands (like paper dolls) in the shape of pumpkins, black cats, scary spooks or bright green frogs.

• Attach small bat shapes to table lamp shades and fit low wattage bulbs to cast an eerie gloom and large shadows. An adult should supervise this before the party.

• Make or buy rustic twig stars and loop together with string, separating each star with a tiny apple to create a simple but effective garland.

• Cover furniture and the tea table with white sheets (or dye black using machine fabric dyes).

• Don't forget to have some spooky music playing to send shivers down your spine.

Spooky Food

Make edible place cards. Cut slices of gingerbread cake into thick chunks and ice on guest names with writing icing. If names are long, write initials only! This is a good activity for the children to do in advance.

After some active games or trick and treating, warm little monsters with a bowl of pumpkin, carrot or tomato soup served with starry toasts. Toast bread as usual (bread should not be too thick). Leave the toast to cool for a second and then use a large star cookie cutter to press out the toasts on a bread board.

The Cake

The most important point about a birthday cake is a great design and presentation with a flourish. Not all party cakes require candles, and personally I think novelty candles (musical and re-lighting versions) are best avoided as they can make younger children over-excited or even upset them. It's far better to concentrate on the design of the cake and have simple coloured cake candles or tiny tapers stuck into holders.

Themed party cakes are simpler to make than you might think and if you are not keen on baking, decorate a shop-bought cake or barter with a friend who likes baking – do a swap with your skills. Try to cut the cake so that every child has a cake decoration or a piece of coloured icing. If you have two similar birthday cakes, one can be pre-cut and wrapped in advance, ready for the goody bags, to save time.

Good relations

Don't force grandparents to attend the party. Some will love to take part in the hustle and bustle. For others who are more elderly or less active, a more sedate family tea at another time would be a better option.

TOP TIP
It's a good idea to plan a couple of extra games or activities to keep up your sleeve in case they are required.

Recording the day

Birthdays are one of the important rites of passage for children and it is great to share the day with relatives that cannot be there. Have one of the adult helpers or an older brother or sister in charge of the camera or video camera and take plenty of shots. Other good options for costume parties include a Polaroid or digital camera, so all the guests can take away a souvenir of the day with them.

AFTER THE EXCITEMENT
Keep a favourite video or two on standby, (nothing too action-packed) to put on at the end of the party in case you have any stragglers who are not collected on time by their parents. This helps your child to come down gently from their birthday-high and also means that you do not have to continue to amuse the children after an exhausting day.

Witch

Wear anything black and make a long, slinky cloak from a square of skirt lining fabric – it's cheap, shiny and usually 140cm (54in) wide. A black bin liner will do as a dress if you cut out neck and arm holes. A black hat, wand and a mean expression are the only extras needed.

Devil

A 150cm (60in) square of red fleece provides a great cover up for little devils and is warm on chilly autumn nights. Add a scary rubber mask or make your own from a paper plate painted red with cut-out eyes and nose, plus some felt horns stuck to a hair band. Make the hair stand in peaks with some hair gel.

Wizard specs

Anyone can look like Harry with these glasses! Take two pipe cleaners. Twist to make a circle in the middle of each for the lenses. Twist two overlapping ends to form the bridge of the glasses. Trim any surplus. The other ends can be curved to fit over the ears. Make sure that there are no sharp ends before wearing.

Goody Bags

Goody bags for guests to take away at the end of the party can be as eagerly awaited as the event itself. When you are having a themed birthday party, it is a great way to round off a memorable party.

When planned in advance, goody bags do not have to be expensive, even when catering for a large number of children. The trick is to hunt out bargain 'presents' over time and be inventive with the presentation. If you buy presents out of season or in sales, the cost can be halved.

To make the goody bags extra-special, think about the presentation. Bought party and gift bags can be expensive, but think of alternatives – purchase small paper carrier bags and customise with paint, stickers and stamps (this is something your child can do to help); sew up mini sacks from a double layer of crêpe paper; use

GOODY BAG CONTENTS

Naturally, the contents will depend on the age group and the theme of the party, but small items with mass appeal include:

- Colourful pencils and pencil toppers
- Key rings
- Paints and brushes
- Craft materials
- Colouring books
- Joke and puzzle books
- Small puzzles
- Tiny toys
- Sweets/lollipops
- Mini photo frames
- Bubble blowers
- Funky pens and pencils
- Decks of cards
- Rubber stamps and stamp pads
- Transfers and stickers
- Small torches
- Balloons
- Scrunchies and hair accessories
- Toiletries and fun bath accessories
- Beads and jewellery kits
- Rubber reptiles and spiders

two large squares of cellophane gathered up like a dolly bag (secure at the top with a rubber band and ribbon). There are loads more ideas within each theme.

Each bag should be labelled with the name of the child to whom it is being given. It is also a good idea to have a couple of spares (or at least spare contents) in case a disaster happens or a younger brother or sister tags along with a party guest.

Halloween Fun

When it's the witching hour, there's nothing like a spooky party to send a delicious shiver down your spine. This is an ideal party for scary costumes and plenty of fun indoor activities, followed by an All Hallows Eve feast.

Gruesome Gareth and Horrible Hattie invite all their spooky friends to a Halloween Party on 31st October at 5.30pm.
Come dressed up as your favourite ghoul, goblin, wizard or witch.

RSVP or we'll send you a slimy toad!
Address
Telephone number

Invitations

• Use purple card covered in gummed stars.

• Make simple potato prints in the shapes of moons, bones or a witch's hat and stamp onto coloured card.

• Stick wobble eyes on some round black circles of card and attach eight long legs (made from pipe cleaners or crêpe paper) to resemble a spider.

• Make a card out of tracing paper and cut a spook shape from white paper to slip between its ghostly covers (write the party details on the reverse).

COSTUMES

Don't rush to buy ready-made costumes from a toy or party shop. Making your own devilish outfit is much more fun and cost effective. In many cases some face paints add the final touch to warty witches or smelly three-eyed monsters.

Wizard

You don't have to go to school to be a wizard. Simply cut stars from some gold and silver card or orange felt and attach to a purple cloak. Decorate a paper cone hat with celestial stickers (use hair grips to secure or have an elastic loop under the chin). A length of dowel painted black, and with silver foil wrapped on the end becomes a magic wand and a hanging bat cut from a square of foam is essential for spells and experiments.

Party Manners

This is not an out-of-date guide to etiquette, but simply some common sense pointers on polite behaviour for guests and hosts, so that the party is enjoyed by all when everyone can be very over-excited.

Guests and their parents

• Do reply to party invitations promptly.
• Remember to advise the host of any food allergies/pet allergies.
• If the party is a costume one, do dress your child up. They will feel left out if all the other guests are warring pirates and Long John Silvers and they are only wearing an eye patch.
• Remind your child to share games and activities and not to be upset if they are not a prize-winner.
• If your child is a fussy eater, encourage them to eat what they like and perhaps try some new food – they may like it!
• Remind your child to say thank you when they leave.
• Do return to collect your child on time. After two hours of frenzied partying, the host will be fit to drop!

Party giver and parents

• Make sure you have assistance from helpers of your choice who will work! This sounds obvious, but unless you are firm with some parents who waft in with their child and offer to help, you'll find yourself organising the birthday party as well as racing around opening wine or making tea for the adults. Politely thank them and say you have plenty of help and little Fiona will be ready for collection at four.
• Make sure your child says thank you for their presents. Remind them that it is not polite to tell their friends if they already have the same book or game, as most presents can be returned to the store.
• Make a note of who gave what when your child unwraps their presents so they can write thank you letters after the party.
• Encourage your child to share their toys with the other children and take turns with games.
• If you have other children, let them take part in the games and tea.

SETTING THE SCENE

- For both French and USA themes red, white and blue is the order of the day. Use plain white china with coloured bowls (France) or heavy diner-style china with oversized mugs and glasses (USA). Napkins can be plain red or blue.

- Paint a white sheet to look like the Tricolour or Stars and Stripes. Alternatively decorate the middle of a plain table cloth with a solid colour red or blue runner. For the 4th July, you can sprinkle paper stars along the runner or twirling ribbons in the style of cheerleaders.

- Finish with miniature flags stuck in traditional, glass cola bottles (USA) or small mineral water or fruit juice bottles (France) filled with sand for stability.

- Instead of placemats, buy a couple of copies of the Wall Street Journal, Le Figaro or other foreign newspaper and place these, folded under the plates.

- Place cards can be decorated with airmail stickers or foreign stamps or can be folded postcards with names written in the style of the theme, such as Monsieur Tom, La Belle Maria, Slick Ben and the Bikers, Anna T and the Pink Ladies.

- Don't forget to have appropriate music playing in the background – Rock'n'Roll from the 50s and 60s to create the atmosphere of an authentic diner or soulful jazz for the feel of the Parisian Left Bank.

- Goody bags are not essential for a brunch party, but if you wish to give guests a little souvenir, these can be placed next to their name cards on the table. Choose anything which is evocative of the theme country.

ACTIVITIES

Why not round off the party with an energetic game of baseball (or rounders) or a more leisurely game of boules? You could present the winning team with baseball caps or berets.

Party Themes

From pirates to princesses and cowboys to explorers – here are some party themes to delight every birthday boy and girl

Summer party

It's great to get together during the long summer holidays. An ideal finishing touch to a birthday sleepover (or before an essential shopping trip with friends) would be a brunch party. Take inspiration from other countries for party themes.

BRUNCH PARTY

A brunch party with a cultural theme can be quite sophisticated and is ideal for older children and teenagers. With luck your son or daughter will be a willing co-party planner with plenty of ideas based on their knowledge of the chosen country, language and culture.

The USA's Independence Day on 4th July is great inspiration for a summer party. You don't necessarily have to be American to celebrate with red, white and blue and it's an easy theme to spark off ideas.

Encourage your guests to come in costume, representing the country – think of Ivy League-type sweatshirts or a sparkly Madonna urban cowboy look. It doesn't have to be full fancy dress, as any accessory such as a stars and stripes flag will help set the scene. Award a prize for the 'best dressed' guest.

Petit Dejeuner French Style

Serve warm croissants and French sticks, continental-style jams, brioches, milky coffee served in bowls or breakfast cups, orange juice, ham and cheese, followed by fruit and yoghurts.

Independence day celebration

Provide muffins, waffles with maple syrup, bacon and eggs-over-easy or sunny-side-up, orange juice, fruit, tea, coffee or milk served in tall glasses or non-spill travel mugs (often given away free by coffee bars).

Choosing a Theme

Choosing a theme is a great way to make any party go with a swing and to give yourself a head start with planning.

Any parent will know what the current dressing-up obsession is with their child and their favourite story themes. Costume parties are the ultimate fantasy for a would-be pirate king or pre-Raphaelite princess. Plus they are great fun for all ages and can encourage unstructured play without the need for constant games or activities. Adult helpers will also enjoy entering into the party spirit and demonstrating their amateur dramatic skills once they are in character!

The following pages show themes which are suitable for both sexes. However, there is no limit to

your imagination – my only advice is, make it easy to interpret into costumes and props. For example, most parents can rustle up a Wild West outfit for little Harry at the drop of a stetson, but dressing up as the Eiffel Tower could demand more time and ingenuity than you may have available!

Discuss with the birthday boy or girl their favourite ideas. Rather than giving them an open choice, perhaps make a shortlist of three from which they can choose. Whatever theme you decide on, you will need to consider costumes, how to set the scene (the 'theatre') with decorations and props, invitations and goody bags. This needs lateral thinking and perhaps a glass of wine to help the ideas flow. A good starting point is to look at children's books. The illustrations are sure to spark off several ideas. Keep making notes over a few days, before you decide on the final plan.

Egg head hats

Sew jolly egg cosies using felt. Cut two shapes, slightly larger than half the circumference of the egg and sew together with contrasting embroidery cottons. Add tassels, beads or buttons depending on what scraps are in your sewing box.

Mad hatters

Create a Mad Hatter's Tea party table with brightly coloured and contrasting table settings. Use crêpe paper for table runners, twirly ribbon and chicken cake decorations at each place setting. Finish off with narcisci, muscari or other spring flowers. Cut stems short and use glass tumblers as low vases, so that they will not get knocked over.

Paper chains

Make seasonal paper chains from coloured paper, tissue or newspaper. Fold long lengths of paper into zigzag sections and draw a motif on the top section. Make sure that the image touches each side of the paper, so that when it is cut out and unfolded, the chain is continuous.

Goody bags

Wrap up some tiny eggs in a pretty paper napkin, tied with a pom-pom like a bunny's tail. Or place eggs in a wicker basket with raffia to resemble a nest or wrap up in a square of netting and a scrap of ribbon. A hot cross bun is always a good seasonal choice, or a sheep-shaped cookie cutter, spring bulbs or summer annuals and of course an egg cup!

ACTIVITIES

Easter egg hunt

This is essential, so hide small chocolate eggs around the garden (or in the house if the weather is not good). The hiding places should not all be obvious, even if this means that you are still coming across the eggs for several days afterwards. Unwrapped eggs can be covered in little twists of

tissue paper or foil tied with scraps of ribbon or raffia. Alternatively, hide coloured boiled eggs wrapped in aluminium foil (see Easter Egg Decorating on page 48).

Miniature garden

Celebrate the spring by making your own tiny garden. Fill a seed tray with soil and 'plant' small bits of vegetation and flower stems in a pleasing design. A handbag mirror makes a good pond and gravel is useful for paths. Keep damp with a water spray and the garden will last for several days.

Count the sweets

Fill a glass jam jar with jelly beans or Smarties and have a 'Guess the number in the jar' competition. The winner, with the closest guess, wins the jar of goodies.

Egg and spoon race

Ideal if the weather allows the children to play in the garden. To make this more difficult, combine with a three-legged race.

Paper cutting

Echo the traditional paper cutting traditions of Poland by folding tissue paper in half and cutting out simple, symmetrical images of chickens, hares, lambs or flowers. Stick onto plain white card or heavy paper to create Easter cards.

Fox and hen game

Choose one player to be a fox. The others form a line, holding each other at the waist. The first in line is the mother hen and the rest are her chicks. The fox tries to catch the last chick in the line. The mother hen protects her chick by barring the fox with his/her outstretched arms. All the chicks help by moving the end of the line away from the fox. When the fox catches a chick, the fox child is rewarded with a chocolate egg and the players choose a new fox and mother hen. If the fox cannot catch a chick within an agreed time, a change around occurs without a prize.

Pirate Party 'Shiver me timbers'

This is a party with plenty of potential and is bound to go down in party folklore in your neighbourhood. Costumes are a breeze to make or adapt from everyday clothes and you can transform your home and garden into a Jolly Roger at the drop of a parrot.

Invitations

There are many options depending on your creative skills. A good idea for many home made invitations is to use folded 'blank' cards available in packs from art and craft shops. Decorate the front and write the party details inside or print out from a computer to save time.

Ideas include a skull and crossbones, paper flags, big canvas knot stuck on 'sailcloth' (calico), illustration by the birthday girl or boy. The invitation can be written as shown here:

Ahoy - me hearties

Cap'n Jack and his trusty crew are sailing into port on 20 July to celebrate his 8th Birthday. Calling all land lubbers to enjoy some swash-buckling fun at his Pirate Party from 4-6.

RSVP
Cap'n Jack
c/o The Jolly Roger
Address
Telephone number

Prizes of booty for the jolliest or most fearsome costumes.

Making Easter bonnets

It is traditional in many countries to wear something new and brightly coloured on Easter Sunday to herald the arrival of spring and the better weather. Making a jazzy Easter bonnet continues this tradition and is also an excellent activity to concentrate young minds for at least 30–45 minutes. Young imaginations don't need much prompting, although it is sure to spark off ideas if adults wear hats prepared earlier. Suggest several shapes that can be made such as a cone shaped bonnet that ties under the chin, a top hat, a mob cap, pill box or a Victorian bonnet. Remember that for Easter bonnets, the rule 'More is Better' definitely applies, so encourage embellishment! Have an Easter parade when everyone is finished and take photographs. Polaroid or digital pictures can be taken away on the day. Alternatively, take a whole roll of film and post a photo to each child later.

Useful materials and decorations

- Coloured card in assorted pastel colours for the hat shapes (enough for one sheet per child)
- Crêpe paper in assorted colours
- Tissue paper (buy this in reams in popular colours such as yellow and pink or buy a multi pack for variety)
- Twirling paper ribbon and scraps of fabric ribbon
- Lengths of longer and wider ribbon (at least 80cm/32in) for the ribbon ties
- Child-safe scissors (one set per child) plus some decorative edge scissors
- Decorative pens or pastel sticks
- Paper doilies
- Glue sticks
- Sequins
- Scraps or squares of felt in assorted colours
- Other useful items – sticky tape (have several reels handy), hole punch, stapler, coloured pens, stamps and stamp pad

A basic bonnet shape

To make the bonnet shown above, see the template on page 63. Re-draw or photocopy the template to size. Fold a piece of card and place the edge marked 'fold' along the folded edge. Cut out the shape. Bring the two edges marked 'overlap' together and staple to form the bonnet shape. Decorate as desired!

COSTUMES

• Wear baggy trousers or shorts in plain colours. If they are old, cut off the bottoms with a zigzag edge.

• Stripy T-shirts with white and black, red or blue stripes are ideal. Paint your own pirate shirt T-shirt with fabric paint (use masking tape to define the stripes and stuff the shirt with paper to prevent the paint soaking through to the other side).

• Heavy leather belts or more fabric tied in a sash around the waist.

• Make a cardboard cutlass and colour it with poster paint.

• Use large brass curtain rings, looped with thread as earrings to loop over the ears.

• Make a newspaper hat for the pirate or make a hat from black art paper with a skull and crossbones stuck on (see folding instructions on page 61).

• Black eye patches.

• Every pirate should wear a bandanna tied around their head. These can be cheap to buy in markets or bargain shops. Alternatively, buy some plain red fabric or gingham and cut into 50cm (20in) squares.

'Ahoy me hearties'

Easter party

An Easter party is an ideal theme for younger children. If you can choose a sunny day, you will be able to organize both indoor and outdoor activities.

Easter egg decorating

Another simple craft that is sure to provide hours of happy entertainment. The children can take their decorated eggs away with them and if you are having an Easter tea, they can also eat boiled eggs that you have coloured earlier.

Remember to only use food dyes on eggs that will be eaten, although decorative eggs can also be coloured using fabric powder dyes. For eggs to be eaten or when working with younger children, hard boil the eggs first. Dilute the food dyes in hot water and add a little salt or white vinegar for permanent colour. Carefully lower the egg into the dye solution and remove when the correct colour is achieved. Drain on kitchen paper and allow to dry on pin stilts (four pins stuck in a polystyrene or cork tile on which the drying egg can be balanced). Alternatively, carefully decorate the raw egg. First blow the egg, by pricking a small hole at either end with a needle and blowing the contents into a bowl. This requires patience and is only recommended for older children. This method only needs to be used if you are planning to keep the fragile decorated eggs. Decorative eggs can also be covered in découpage papers, stamps, stickers, foils, sequins and ribbons.

For an Easter party theme, the most important ingredients are eggs of course, both chocolate ones and hens' eggs, but don't forget there are many other types of egg, including goose or quail eggs if you can get them. Papier mâché eggs from craft supply shops are also great for decorating. The only other items you will need to stock pile are crafts materials — see the list opposite for ideas. Remember you can never have too many glue sticks!

Invitations

Have fun making combined Easter cards/invitations. There are plenty of sources of inspiration – rabbits, chicks, eggs and egg-cups. Cut shapes from felt or coloured paper and decorate with stickers, paint or scraps of ribbon.

Pirate place settings

- Use a plain coloured oil cloth or white paper table cloth with a big red cross made of crêpe paper or fabric.
- Make place mats from coloured paper with circles, squares or triangles to look like nautical flags.
- Have plain or stripy red or black napkins. Place cards can have names such Pirate Nimble Nancy or Pirate Slippery Sam.

Outdoor Fun
- Set up a hammock if possible.
- Make an awning from some calico or an old sheet. Tie each corner to four sturdy poles and make guy ropes to keep the poles vertical. (Use tent poles and guys if you already have them.) You can either set up the birthday tea table underneath or put down some blankets and cushions and have a swash-buckling pirate story-telling session.

SETTING THE SCENE

Treasure chest

Any toy chest can be turned into a treasure chest. (Disguise if necessary by painting or by wrapping in brown or gold crêpe paper.) Prop it open and bulk out with a blanket. Cover the top with more crêpe or tissue paper. Drape old jewellery over, or place chocolate coins and any other booty, such as sports trophies (real or plastic), compasses, friendship bracelets, at the top.

Nautical bunting

Make nautical bunting from coloured paper or scraps of fabric and sew or staple onto seam binding. Pin to the washing line or festoon around the house.

Pirate flag

Using some plain black fabric, cut out a rectangle for a flag at least 30cm x 45cm, (12in x 18in) stick on a felt skull and crossbones, or use a fusible web (such as Bondaweb) to iron on one in white fabric. Attach to a bamboo pole and drive into the ground. If you make several, plant one near the front gate. See templates on pages 59 and 60.

Celebrate the coming summer with a nature walk followed by a picnic in the garden. Set the scene with a brightly coloured picnic rug, piled with comfortable cushions and a simple afternoon tea of jam sandwiches, traditional cakes, fruit salad and lemonade.

Or why not have a midwinter party to celebrate the winter solstice and the shortest day? Choose a non-Christmas theme and colour scheme as children can get overloaded with red and green at this time of year. What about a black and white penguin party? Ask all the guests to come in black and white clothes and decorate the party room to look suitably Antarctic with white and turquoise crêpe paper, clear cellophane and white card, cut out to look like icebergs.

Have craft activities such as making a wacky bow tie for their 'penguin outfit', making penguin masks, painting jam jars with glass paints to make decorative tea light holders, or decorating small fairy cakes with chocolate, white glacé icing and coloured jelly shapes (this is always hugely popular with boys and girls of a variety of ages). Incorporate any games to do with fish and finish up with a suitable story about marine life or famous explorers, depending on their age. Don't forget evocative music is so important – have nature CDs (of the wind or dolphins) playing, in order to create the right mood.

GAMES AND ACTIVITIES

• **Sack race** – See page 23.

• **3-legged Long John Silver race.**

• **Pirate hats** – make from newspaper against the clock. Give a quick demonstration and then let each guest make up their own (see template on page 61).

• **Treasure hunt** – give the guests clues or a map leading them around the garden to points with signs such as Cannibal Cove, Pegleg Point, Crocodile Swamp. At the final point, have one big prize for the winner and consolation prizes (chocolate coins) for the runners up.

• **Pin the Beak on the Parrot** – (variation of Pin the Tail on the Donkey).

• **Make a telescope** – Before the party save toilet rolls or kitchen rolls (get friends and neighbours to help with this!). Cover one end with coloured cellophane. Stick down or secure with a rubber band. Cover with a piece of white paper and get the children to decorate with coloured pens. This is a good game to quieten things down or to use as an opener as guests arrive.

• **Losers to competitive games** – They can choose to walk the plank or take a booby prize such as lemon drops or other eek-inducing sweets. For the plank, balance a narrow plank above a paddling pool and blindfold the victim. Turn them around a couple of times before getting them to walk to the other side. Have towels on standby! If you have a slide, place the pool at the bottom. This type of activity must be supervised by an adult or two.

• **Throw the Rats Overboard** – Make up rats from old grey socks filled with rice or lentils and fastened with rubber bands. Have a tail of wool hanging out the end and stick on wobbly eyes. See how far the children can throw them.

Goody bags

• Cut up a black bin liner and resew or tape into smaller goody sacks. Stick on a photocopied skull and crossbones. Tie at the top with some coloured ribbon or fabric.
• Cut cream calico into squares (like sails) and knot at the top with thick string or thin rope.
• Ideas for contents: plastic jewellery plundered from the treasure chest, silver or gold chocolate coins, oranges (to prevent scurvy on long sea voyages), glass bottles of cola relabelled 'Best Navy Rum', any of the props they may have been given when dressing up.

Parties For All Seasons

Celebrating the changing seasons is a great excuse for a party! Birthdays are always eagerly awaited but even if you don't have a special occasion to celebrate, seasonal parties such as Halloween are a wonderful way to rediscover and enjoy traditional crafts and games. Children will love to spend time before the party helping you to prepare the games and food.

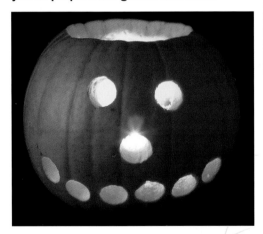

On the following pages are ideas for parties to fit the main school holidays. However, think up your own themes to suit the age and likes of your child. For example, as a change from a standard princess party, why not organise a May Day party? You can make an impromptu maypole by decorating a rotary washing line – simply wrap the vertical pole in strips of red and white crêpe paper and have plenty of coloured streamers hanging down. Or for an authentic maypole, paint a length of cardboard carpet tube white and attach ribbons or strips of gingham firmly to the top. Get the children to make up dances that interweave the ribbons, thus wrapping the pole.

Sporty Party

A sports-themed party is ideal for energetic youngsters and will encourage them to burn off some of their never-ending energy. This party theme is ideal for older children, of eight years plus, where they can be actively involved with the planning of activities and decorations.

'We are the champions!'

Invitations

If you have a football-mad child, make card invitations in the shape of a football strip (use coloured card to copy their favourite team). Make a template to trace around. Your child's age can be written or stuck on like a player's number. Or make invitations in the shape of a rugby or tennis ball, football trophy or swimming costume (add stickers for a spotty costume). As this will be an activity-based party, it is a good idea for guests to wear shorts, T-shirts and trainers, so mention this on the invitation.

BE A GOOD SPORT

All sporting champions
are invited to
David's 9th Birthday Party
at the sports centre in
(town name)
on 10th September at 2.30
followed by an Olympic feast at home.

RSVP
David Hat-Trick Smith
Address
Telephone number

Wear shorts and trainers/Bring
a swimming costume and towel
(or whatever is appropriate)

Seasonal Parties

**Celebrate the changing
seasons with exciting
parties and fun activities**

SETTING THE SCENE

The simplest option if you have a local sports centre or swimming pool, is to use this as the party venue. Many now hire out pools or pitches for birthdays, with a choice of activities such as circuit training or indoor soccer.

Make sure you discuss the choice of sports with the birthday child – they will, of course, want to play their favourites! It may be easier to hire a mini-bus to transport all the partygoers to and from your home, so that guests don't go astray looking for the party venue. Other more unusual options include a bowling alley or ice skating rink. If this is not an option because of distance or cost – do not despair – your home can easily be converted into an Olympic stadium at minimal effort and expense.

GAMES AND ACTIVITIES

As prizes for games, why not make some quick winners' rosettes out of gathered strips of crêpe paper stuck behind a circle of card? Try to ensure that each child receives a rosette during the party.

Fourth Division

A great icebreaker as guests arrive. Prepare four-part 'jigsaws' of famous sports personalities (use photographs from newspapers or magazines). Try to use similar sizes of images, or photocopy to a similar size. Cut into four. Randomly hand out four parts of different puzzles to each child. The children have to circulate quickly and swap parts. The first to make a whole picture is the winner. Give each guest an extra point for the name of the sportsman or woman.

Setting the scene

With such a wealth of artistic talent at your disposal, let the party crowd decorate their own party table. A plain white paper tablecloth can be transformed with crayons, potato printing and hand prints. If you do this as soon as they arrive, it will have a chance to dry before the birthday tea. Give each child a plain white fabric napkin to be decorated with fabric crayons – the colours are fixed by ironing which should be supervised by an adult. Paper cups can be decorated with stickers and paper shapes.

TOP TIP!

Children spend a lot of their time 'being organized' by others at home and school. They will be quite happy, once any techniques or do's and don'ts have been explained, to get on with craft activities on their own.

Edible Art

Make marzipan fruits. Divide the marzipan between the children. Make a small hollow in the marzipan, add a couple (only a couple!) of drops of food colouring and continue to knead until the colour mixes in. Knead the marzipan to soften and roll into small balls. Decorate with cloves, angelica as mini stems or dust lightly in icing sugar for peaches. Paint stripes on bananas with brown food colouring and create a textured surface on oranges by rolling the fruit on a cheese grater. Admire and eat at the birthday tea!

Games and Activities

For a party lasting a maximum of two hours you will only need a couple of different activities. Have a mix of imaginative work (painting or drawing), messier creative work (salvage crafts, T-shirt printing, collage, modelling, stamping or hand printing) plus a one or two active party games to keep the inspiration flowing.

Ask a creative adult or teenage friend along to help out. Remember it's a party not an art lesson and the emphasis is on fun. All children will enjoy drawing using charcoal, drawing with their left hand (if right handed), drawing without taking their pencil from the sheet, blowing up balloons and drawing funny faces on them with felt tip pens or drawing using pencils or brushes attached to long sticks – all these games are easy to organize and are a hoot to try.

DRAW A COW

The players must draw a cow whilst blindfolded. Starting with the eyes the players must draw a feature, drop their hand, pause, then draw another feature and so on. The winner can be the child whose cow is most recognizable but have a fun prize for the funniest drawing.

Goody bags

These are easy to fill with the creations made during the afternoon. You can also include a fabric crayon, a paintbrush, small pack of pencils, hopscotch chalks, glitter glue or stickers.

Match tie

A picture game in which flash cards of equipment (football, golf club) have to be matched up to the sport. Cut out pictures from sports magazines or download pictures from the Internet or clip art software. Try to include some more unusual sports for older children. To make this more active, children can sit in a line with the names of the sports laid around the room/garden or pinned on the washing line, for the children to grab.

Goody Bags

Why not try to imitate sports bags with drawstring bags sewn from brightly coloured rip stop nylon or jersey (or look for cheap pencil cases)? Fill with high-energy drinks or snack bars, fruit juices and shoe laces, skipping ropes, chalk for hopscotch, sports stickers or swap cards. Check sports shops for other pocket money ideas.

Goal!

This is very active, indoors or out! It can be played in heats to find an eventual winner. Give two balloons to each player – one round and one long. The round balloons should be different colours so they do not get confused. Each player uses the long balloon as a bat and tries to dribble or hit the round balloon into the goal (a cardboard box or laundry basket) at the far end of the room. The first to score a goal is the winner of that heat.

Sack race

Some of the most traditional games are still the best. Get some hessian sacks from a local greengrocer or farmer, or sew some sacks using fabric from the remnant bin of a fabric or furnishing store. Depending on how many sacks are available and the number of party guests, the races can be run in heats or as a relay race with children hopping to a fixed point and then swapping with a team mate.

Arty Party

Children of all ages enjoy being creative and are eager to have a go at new arts and crafts. If you have creative friends, pull them in to help or to give some impromptu tuition.

Preparation

Start hoarding raw materials well in advance. Essential equipment in your creative crafts box (useful throughout the year, not just at party times) can include a variety of white and coloured papers for drawing, painting or sticking; child-safe scissors; foam sheets; wacky pipe cleaners; glue sticks; felt squares; paints; brushes; crayons; PVA glue; sticky tape and face paints.

Have plenty of newspaper for covering tables. Remember that prevention is easier than stain removal! For fabric painting, you can buy plain white cotton napkins and some white T-shirts.

Invitations

Photocopy the outline of an artist's palette for the invitations for the birthday child to add the paint colours. Or buy a pack of art postcards and write the invitation on the reverse, or attach a print out with the party details. Remember to state clearly on the invitation that activities may be messy, so children should wear play clothes and bring an apron or old shirt as a cover up. Have some extra shirts on stand-by, just in case.

Peter is inviting all his artistic chums to his studio for an Arty Party to celebrate his 8th Birthday. Wear old clothes (berets and smocks optional!) and create your own masterpiece to take away on the day. The fun takes place at 2.30 on 13th March.

RSVP
Peter Picasso Jones
Address
Telephone number

Cipher sports

A good game for cooling down before food or going home. Encode the attached list for each guest. Each code unravels to spell out a sport (or sports personality). To encode the words, or to make up more suggestions, remove vowels, make alternative letters jump by one letter, or turn into anagrams.

The children have to work out and write down the correct names. Explain the code breaking methods to the children before they start. For example, badminton becomes bdmntn (vowels removed), lacrosse becomes madrpste (jumping alternative letters), football becomes float lob (anagram).

ANSWERS: GOLF, SKIING, ROWING

cricket
rowing
football
tiddlywinks
cross country skiing
tennis
horse racing
speedway
lacrosse
ice hockey
salsa dancing
rugby union
down hill bobsleigh
formula 1 racing
basketball
curling
ping pong
athletics
swimming
badminton

Fantasy football and design-a-jockey

Design a new football strip for your fantasy team or racing silks for your own stable. Photocopy and enlarge the drawings shown below and get children to colour in patterns and colours of their choice. Have plenty of inexpensive colouring pens on hand. Buy packs of coloured sticky stars and spots from stationers for the racing silks. Give a prize for the most outlandish outfit.

KIDS' COCKTAILS

A fun activity is to have an adult bartender mixing up exotic concoctions for party guests. The essential features for any cocktail are a dramatic name, outrageous colour and fun accessories including neon coloured bendy straws, cocktail umbrellas and garnishes of fruit, such as pineapple, orange, banana, seedless grapes and kiwi fruit. Create dramatic dyed icecubes with food colouring. Limequats (baby limes) can be sliced into two and frozen as an alternative ice cube. Use brightly coloured acrylic or plastic tumblers and these can be included in the goody bags after washing.

Remember that fizzy children's drinks are usually available sugar-free and additive-free, but as an alternative you can always colour lemonade with food colourings.

Sundowner

Pour pure orange juice into a tall glass. Gently pour in some cranberry juice. The red fruit juice slowly works through the orange producing a dramatic sunset effect.

Lime Time

This can be limeade or apple juice served 'straight up'. Garnish with green accessories and green grapes, apple chunks and kiwi slices.

Red Alert

For a traffic-stopping drink, first place in the glass a strawberry, then slice of orange, green grape and so on until the glass is almost full. Slowly pour on cherryade so that it soaks through the layers. Provide an umbrella or spoon so that the traffic light fruit can be scooped up and eaten.

Blue Lagoon

First dip the rim of the glass in lemon juice and then press the upturned glass into coloured sugar (using sugar shaken with food colouring in a jam jar). Colour lemonade with blue food colouring. Wrap the top end of a long kebab skewer with a strip of green crêpe paper, stick with a tiny piece of clear tape and fringe to look like a palm tree. Thread the skewer with pineapple, orange and pineapple chunks and pop into the drink just before serving.

Great Explorers' Party

For energetic children of all ages, an explorers' party is bound to appeal to their sense of adventure and is a brilliant excuse to have the party out-of-doors. Ask guests to wear jeans, shorts or old clothes.

Invitations

Cut up some old maps and stick to cards. Randomly mark a big red X on the cards and draw the points of a compass. Or stick leaves onto a card with the party details.

Dr Livingstone presumes you would like to come to a party to celebrate Lucy's 10th birthday. The great adventure takes place on 23rd August at 4pm in the swamps and tropical rainforests of her garden. Daring explorers can bring a sleeping bag and sleep out under the stars.

RSVP: Lucy Livingstone
Address
Telephone
Map attached so you can find the way!

BEACH PARTY FOOD AND DRINKS

Food can be barbecued or prepared in the kitchen and served on skewers (chicken satay sticks or fruit kebabs are always popular). Serve exotic-looking non-alcoholic cocktails or fruit smoothies in tall glasses with garnishes, umbrellas and bendy straws. Use brightly coloured paper tableware or plastic and acrylic partyware. Remember that clashing colours and patterns are the desired effect.

For a Bali-high atmosphere, eat the birthday tea seated on cushions around a low table near the ground. With older children, it is probably safe to have candles in containers or hanging lanterns.

Ice-cream parlour

Another birthday tea treat that is always popular is to set up a pretend ice-cream parlour. You'll need at least half a dozen soft scoop ice-cream varieties of different colours such as chocolate, mint choc chip, toffee, strawberry, raspberry ripple and lemon sorbet. Don't forget the old favourite vanilla for good measure. Buy an assortment of wafer fans, chocolate wafer curls and coloured sprinkles, fruit toppings and chopped nuts (be careful of food allergies) and have bowls of fruit such as sliced bananas, raspberries and peaches. Let the children choose their combination of fruit, ice-cream and toppings and serve in classic pressed glass sundae dishes or brightly coloured picnicware with long-handled spoons.

SETTING THE SCENE

This is really an outdoor party, so is ideal for summer holidays. Remember your garden is no longer a lawn and flower beds, but an exciting adventure playground in which children can let off steam and use up energy!

• Set up various tents dotted around the lawn – use instant pop-out tents, pup tents and old sheets or blankets slung over clothes horses or washing lines.

• Firmly tie two lines of stout rope, one above the other between two trees, so that kids can walk across.

• Use a sturdy kitchen table (not a trestle table) as a look-out post. Drive long bean poles into the ground at each corner and lash together with bunting or throw a camouflage net (or old net curtain dyed or painted) over the top.

• Put on a tape or CD of jungle music or wildlife noises. Hide the CD player under bushes.

• Make signs saying CAUTION! WILD BEARS, DO NOT FEED THE TIGERS and DO NOT WORRY THE SHEEP. Prop soft toys next to the signs.

Other sources of inspiration

• This party can be a real mix of cultures, so if you live somewhere which has Indian textile stores or Oriental supermarkets, look there for ideas – inexpensive saris for use as tablecloths, paper Chinese lanterns, incense sticks.

• Check out sports stores and fashion shops, specialising in 'surf style' for ex-display material that you may be able to recycle (full-size palm trees for example!).

• Look in travel brochures for other ideas on colours and motifs.

Goody bags
Use crêpe paper sacks filled with small blow-up plastic balls, tropical fruit drinks, diving goggles, shells, exotic hair clips and funny sunglasses. Teenagers could receive a fragrant tealight and holder or a lip balm tied up in a wisp of dyed muslin or net.

'In the summertime when the weather is fine'

GAMES AND ACTIVITIES

Many of the activities involve unstructured play, which allows adults some respite.

Adventurer

Tie ropes with a knot onto strong branches as improvised swings. To add some excitement, have a jumping off point, a paddling pool in the centre and landing 'mat' on the other side. Be prepared for wet clothes as some children inevitably jump in!

Scavenger hunt

First split the children up into small teams. Provide a series of numbered written clues or directions leading to crossed sticks, pebbles set in a pattern, sun dials or leaves anchored down with stones. Subsequent clues are at each point (write on the backs of maps or dye paper in tea to look like old charts) or print out on the computer with the clue hidden by a load of gobbledegook. Have small prizes for each team member.

Bug catching

Devise a game where explorers have to catch the most interesting insect – have a book to hand to enable identification and encourage players to make up a story about the adventure they had when they were hunting for the rare insect in the jungle.

Relay race

Divide into two teams. When it's your turn put on the rucksack, run to a point and pick up an object (wild animal stuffed toy, map, compass, sleeping bag etc), put it into the rucksack, run back and pass the rucksack to the next member of the team.

The stalking game

Have quiet stalking games with the 'hunter' blind-folded.

Sleeping lions

This is a great game for trying to quieten over-excited guests before the meal or going home time. Everyone has to lie completely still. The first to wriggle or make a noise is out and then helps the judge to check the other contestants (tickling is good for provoking a response!).

Cunning clothes pegs

A good game for young children is hunt the coloured clothes peg. These are pegged to leaves, washing lines, flower pots and other more hidden locations. Each child has to gather as many as possible and perhaps one of each colour, within a time limit. For older children, make a list with pictures of different leaves, flowers or birds. Attach photocopies of the different items with clothes pegs as before. Each child has to collect the full set of pictures and match up correctly to the list. (Use a child's encyclopedia or CD-ROM for ideas and lists.)

GAMES AND ACTIVITIES

Beach relay races

Divide into two teams. Each contestant has to run to a marker, then run around this three times holding onto the pole and with their head bent. When they try to run back they'll be very wobbly, having run round in circles!

Flap the Fish

Cut small fish shapes from light-weight paper (tissue paper is ideal). Cut eight 10cm (4in) 'flappers' from cards. Rather like tiddlywinks, the object is to flap the fish along the ground to the finishing line by creating a draught. Divide into teams with timed heats, or have a general free-for-all.

Coconut shy

Set up various targets – they don't all have to be coconuts! Each target can be marked with a different number of points depending on how difficult it is to hit with the ball. Each player throws four balls and the winner is the child with the highest score who may then choose a prize. Prizes could include funny sunglasses, floral hair accessories, small packs of coloured pencils or crayons, or a small tube of sunscreen.

Dancing

Hawaiian dancing and limbo dancing are always popular activities. Boys and girls will enjoy a lively limbo dancing competition to the sound of Caribbean music.

Team Games

Volleyball, badminton and beach skittles are all good outside games.

On the towel

The old standby of 'on the rug, off the rug' can be given a tropical twist with a brightly coloured beach towel or two. This burns up a lot of energy jumping on and off and can be repeated as it is a quick time filler for five minutes.

Essential explorers' equipment

For an outdoor adventure party, practical clothing is a must, especially if you are going for a walk. Don't forget waterproofs, a fleece for warmth, comfortable shoes and a sun hat (remember to put these requirements on the invitation). Other good ideas are binoculars, a compass, a disposable camera or two and a magnifying glass so everyone can be involved. Children should also have a rucksack in which you can put iron rations such as a bottle of drink, some fruit and biscuits. Adults accompanying the explorers should also take sun tan lotion, a map and a mobile phone.

Animal masks

An ideal activity for rainy days when explorers cannot play in the garden. You can make a whole zoo of wild animals! They are made from paper plates and bowls, empty salad or yoghurt pots (especially those ones with divided corners for fruit), egg boxes, tissue paper, straws and crêpe paper. Staple the muzzles onto the plate and stick or glue egg boxes or circles for the eyes (this can be done in advance).

Children can stick on tissue and crêpe paper to decorate the noses and faces. Scrunched up tissue looks like fur and strips of paper make great whiskers. Paint on eyes with poster paint. For ears, cut a circle from paper, make a snip from the edge to the centre and overlap to form a curved ear. Staple to the plate.

The fishing game

Cut tropical fish from brightly coloured paper. Give each fish different scores, e.g. 5, 10, 25. Stick on a small fridge magnet (available in packs from art and craft suppliers). Make a fishing rod from a stick with a string and magnet attached. Throw all the fish onto a sheet of blue paper (the 'Blue Lagoon'). Contestants each have to fish in turn against the clock. Highest score wins.

Setting the scene

'Summertime and the living is easy'

• Have bunting, balloons or crêpe paper chains everywhere to create a festive spirit.

• Cover a garden umbrella with raffia strands and suspend outdoor fairy lights or snaking lights from the spokes.

• Have suitable music for the age group — this can be anything from reggae, the latest 'summer holiday' hits, summertime classics or salsa!

• Using artificial flowers, string up some hanging flower gardens.

• Present every guest on arrival with a garland (bought from party and carnival shops) or make some crêpe paper flowers, strung onto a length of thread or ribbon.

Costumes

• Hawaiian skirts can be made from fringed crêpe paper, brown paper or raffia attached to a ribbon or tape waistband.

• Mermaids can wear a bikini or swimming costume. Tie a 2m length of coloured nylon net and muslin around your waist. The excess length acts as a fish tail. Wear fancy flip flops.

• Surf dudes can wear bright shorts and loud Hawaiian print shirts.

• Simple sarong skirts can be made from a rectangle of fabric knotted around the waist.

• Carmen Miranda (this is a good one for adult helpers!) with plenty of plastic fruit piled up as a head-dress.

Goody bags

Make goody bags from camouflage material, old maps folded and stuck to form paper bags, or jungle print paper. The contents can include anything which encourages adventure – small compass, energy or cereal snack bars, pull-top bottles of spring water, book of adventure stories, snapstick light (available from camping stores), thick 'hiking' socks, tiny travel toothbrush/toothpaste (get a frequent traveller to collect freebies on plane journeys!) plus a notebook and twig pencil for recording tales of daring adventure.

Explorers' rations

Food can be a picnic or barbecue. Having a bonfire for toasting marshmallows or similar and hot chocolate is always a winner. Serve food on leaf plates and bowls (available at Asian supermarkets).

Make an explorers' camp

For a small group of older children (over tens), extend the fun by sleeping out under the stars or in a tent. This separates the men from the boys as the family cat or local hedgehog is bound to produce squeals and shrieks and the average suburban garden at night suddenly seems like a vast forest miles from civilization.

Tropical Beach Party

Even if you don't live in an all-year-round summer climate, with a little imagination even the suburbs can look exotically tropical.

Invitations

Some ideas for home-made cards are to cut and stick some triangular felt pennants or shells onto a card; simply tie some raffia around some brightly coloured card; use a colourful artificial flower, with a note attached to its stem; use glossy pictures cut from a travel brochure.

The essential element is colour and plenty of it. Think magenta, hot orange, lime green, citrus yellow and sky blue and you are already halfway there. This theme is easily adapted to an under-the-sea theme if you prefer.

Limbo down to Lucy's Beach Party on 15 July from 11.00 til 1.30. Come as a mermaid, surfer or anything totally tropical and have some sun-filled fun.

RSVP to
Lucy Grenadine
Address
Telephone number

'Dr Livingstone, I presume?'

Other sources of inspiration

• Army surplus stores for fancy dress.

• Camping and outdoor adventure stores.

• Very young children will enjoy a wild safari. Hide lots of soft animal toys in the garden for them to find.

• Older children will get the same high with an orienteering event, arranged in the local park. Remember to have plenty of adult helpers at the check-in points with mobile phones and set strict boundaries (i.e. within the park).

• For teenagers, war games or paint balling sessions are ideal. These can be arranged indoors or outside. Look up Paintball and Combat Games in the telephone directory.

Ranch food for hungry cowhands

Whether you are eating indoors or outdoors, make the meal seem like a picnic. Sit on old tree stumps or old cushions around a bonfire if outside. Suspend lanterns from punched tin cans from the trees at dusk. Indoors, keep it simple by covering the table in a white sheet decorated with black fabric paint to look like a cow hide. Food should be hearty and simple – bangers from a barbecue, baked potatoes and baked beans.

Serve on paper plates with checkered napkins, or use enamel plates and swig 'moonshine' from enamel mugs (available from camping stores). Once washed, these can go into the goody bags.

TOP TIP

Many children prefer savoury to sweet food. The birthday cake can be the sweet element and can always be cut up and put in the goody bag after a filling barbecue. However, remember the lighting of the candles and singing 'Happy Birthday' is essential, even for rough-tough cowhands.

Goody bags

•Why not cut up old denim jeans (or buy for a song from charity shops) and whizz up into pouches using a sewing machine?
• Use cheap bandannas knotted as a swag bag. The scarf is then a major part of the goody bag
• Use mock suede or chamois leathers to make bag fringes and attach to more conventional brown paper bags.
• Contents: water pistols, friendship bracelets, beads, feathers and a length of leather cord to make Native American-style jewellery.

Princesses and Sleepovers

All children believe they are beautiful princesses or daring knights. Encourage this imaginative play with a princess party which can continue long into the night with a sleepover.

ACTIVITIES

Princess and the pea

The peas are ping pong balls. Two players take part and the object of the game is to collect as many peas as possible. Throw the peas (use about fifteen) about the room. At one end there are two chairs with small bowls. Each player has a spoon and picks up the balls without using their other hand and fills their bowl. An alternative is to suck through straws to pick up the ping pong balls. The winner is the child with the greatest number of peas.

Story princess

Any adult who is a good story teller can take on this role. Dress up as a medieval princess and sit on a decorated throne. All the children gather round and are told a story. You can alternate between stories that invite audience participation and updated classics that could quieten things down at the end of the party.

Setting the Scene

You want to create the illusion of a fairytale world. This can be done inside or out and the magic ingredient is a large amount of nylon netting. This costs pennies, so be generous with quantities.

Hang from the ceiling to create a tented look. Create a princess throne by painting or spraying a junk shop chair in gold and swathe with a cheap feather boa. Wrap cushions in squares of satin lining fabric and tie opposite ends to secure. Cover the tea table with a paper cloth and decorate with a satin runner, cheap sari or confetti and a layer of net on top. Mood music is vital to set the scene.

As guests arrive, let them each choose from the dressing up box of frippery – ballerina tutus, chiffon scarves and lengths of satin lining. Wands and tiaras are essential – ensure there is one for each guest (these can be taken home after the party).

GAMES

- Have a pow-wow, sitting in a circle with a story.

- Lasso the cow (variation on hoopla). Have various soft toys dotted about the grass. Each contestant has to try to lasso one with a looped rope. Alternatively, in a confined space, use a stetson instead of a lasso.

- Beading, beadloom weaving or making friendships bracelets.

- Archery competition.

- Make a feather head-dress.

- Make a bead and seed picture. Using child-safe glue on a card background, use lentils and seeds to create a simple picture.

- Winners of games can be given a sheriff's badge cut from gold card.

- Organise a barn dance with country music and square dancing.

- Paint a totem pole. Photocopy an outline onto A3 paper for the guests to colour in (this is a good opener for when guests arrive).

TERRIFIC TOTEM

Totem poles are created by Native Americans and include commemorative carved images of notable people, plus animals and birds with which the community felt a particular allegiance. Make your own using a cardboard tube, about 12cm (5in) in diameter and 1.8m tall (carpet stores will give these tubes away for free).

Paint with poster paint and add a curling snake detail. The Big Chief Thunderbird, eagle and wild bear are all cut from cardboard boxes, using the templates on page 62 and painted. Cut a slot in the top of the pole for the totem head to slide into. Stick an extra rectangle of card with four notches cut out, to the reverse of the eagle and bear motifs. Loop an elastic band around two notches, position at the right height on the totem and loop the band around the remaining notches.

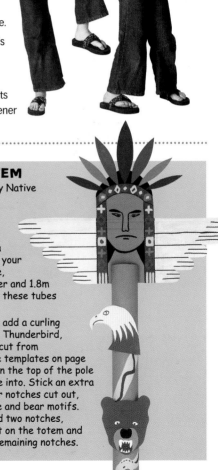

Slumber parties

An ideal activity for girls is a beauty salon makeover, in which they can style their hair and apply simple make-up such as nail polish, lip gloss and body glitter. Remember to have plenty of cotton wool and make-up remover to hand!

Another idea is a DIY Fashion Show. Provide white bin bags, masses of crêpe paper, sticky tape, scissors, feathers and other trimmings. Have a time limit and challenge each guest to come up with an original outfit.

Some sort of craft activity is always a good idea, such as bead jewellery making or decorating boxes with jewels and trimmings as treasure boxes. Why not have a fashion parade and record each model on film?

To try and settle them before bed – have a video which they can watch tucked up in their sleeping bags or duvets. However, be prepared for plenty of chatting, giggling, midnight feasts and very little sleep!

OTHER IDEAS

How about a castle party? This is particularly good for a mixed group of boys and girls. Get four large cardboard boxes from your local electrical or furniture store. Cut to form a castellated profile for the four towers. Stretch corrugated card or brown paper between the towers. Activities can include dressing up as knights in crêpe paper tabards or damsels in conical hats, painting shields, and charging around as jousting knights. Have an archery tournament with sucker-type arrows. As an alternative to a castle, create a tented pavilion (adapt summer canvas gazebos), decorated with pennants and plenty of cushions.

Goody bags

For a princess party, make up dolly bags from several layers of net or tissue paper and clear cellophane. Contents should be sparkly wherever possible. Ideas for gifts include small jewellery bead kits; glitter glue and small notebooks; inexpensive plastic jewellery; sparkle hair or body glitter; pretty pastel coloured sweets; lamé scrunchies and tiaras; bath cubes; lip gloss and hair gel.

Setting the scene

• Use some bean poles lashed together and covered in a three-quarters-circle of calico as an instant teepee. Include props such as leather boots, coils of rope, denim jackets and perhaps even a bale of straw!

• Make 3D cacti from large painted cardboard boxes obtained from furniture or electrical stores. Paint them, then glue on pom poms to look like cactus flowers.

• Have checked blankets or Aztec-type rugs dotted around.

This is a Parragon book
This edition published in 2005

Parragon
Queen Street House
4 Queen Street
Bath, BA1 1HE, UK

This edition designed by
Design Principals, Warminster

Text by Marion Haslam
Edited by Gillian Haslam
Photography by Roddy Paine

ISBN 1-40544-370-7
Printed in China

Marion Haslam
A freelance writer and editor of *Popular Patchwork* magazine, Marion greatly enjoys seasonal and birthday celebrations, plus the planning and 'theatre' of a successful party. Previously a buyer for several design-led retailers in the UK and abroad, Marion is also the author of *Retro Style — 50s Decorating for Today* in association with *Living etc* magazine. Other family craft books include *My Bead Box* and *Spooky Fun*.

DISCLAIMER
· Young children should always be supervised by a responsible adult when making the craft and food items described in this book. Adults should ensure that activities are properly set up and supervised to ensure safety and enjoyment for the party giver and guests.
· Candles are an important part of birthday traditions. Remember never to place or light candles near paper decorations, or leave lit candles unattended. Always ask an adult to light candles and place nightlights in a suitable container. If using fairy lights to decorate the garden, make sure that they are suitable for outdoor use.
· Young children should never be left unsupervised if potentially dangerous implements such as knives or scissors are in use.
· Every effort has been taken to make the instructions clear and accurate.
· The author, publisher and their agents cannot accept liability for any loss, damage, illness or injury however caused.

Wild Wild West Party

For a birthday party at home on the range, a Wild West theme with sheriffs, Native Americans plus law-dodging cowboys and cowgirls is guaranteed to raise the roof of any domestic saloon. So for a hoedown with plenty of yee-hah, read on!

Costumes

It's so simple to ride into the OK Corral – jeans, sturdy belts and checked shirts or sweat shirts are all that's needed from the cupboard, with the addition of a toy-store stetson and a bandanna (re-use a plaid napkin) tied around the neck. Alternatively fringe a 40cm (16in) square of checked fabric. Have some spares for guests.

If you are feeling adventurous, make a fringed 'leather' waistcoat from some brown felt or some chaps from some fake fur fabric tied around the waist. Make a sheriff's badge from gold card.

Invitations

Stick a feather or length of fringed felt on the card, draw a cactus, a sheriff's badge or a teepee and write as follows:

Lone Ranger Richard wants to round up all Ranch Hands for a Wild West Party.

Calling all Cowgirls and Boys, Squaws and Big Chiefs to the Birthday Reservation

on 10 August from 2 to 4.30.

RSVP in writing or by smoke signals to:
Lone Ranger Richard
c/o The OK Corral
Address
Telephone number